Jeremy Noel-Tod

THE WHITSUN WEDDING VIDEO
A Journey into British Poetry

Jeremy Noel-Tod

THE WHITSUN WEDDING VIDEO
A Journey into British Poetry

Rack Press Editions

Rack Press Editions is an imprint of Rack Press Poetry

Typeset by CB editions, London
Printed by the Dorset Press

Published in Wales by Rack Press,
The Rack, Kinnerton, Presteigne, Powys, LD8 2PF
Tel: 01547 560 411
All orders and correspondence:
rackpress@nicholasmurray.co.uk

ISBN 978-0-9931045-4-1

For Robert Potts and Graeme Richardson

The best contemporary poetry can give us a feeling of excitement and a sense of fulfilment different from any sentiment aroused even by very much greater poetry of a past age.

T. S. Eliot

There are few things more disturbing than the realization that we are becoming a nation of minor poets.

P. G. Wodehouse

If you go to a football game you don't have to understand it in any way except the football way.

Gertrude Stein

Contents

ACKNOWLEDGEMENTS

Some of the following opinions first appeared in the *Daily Telegraph,* the *Guardian*, the *New Statesman*, the *Sunday Times* and the *Times Literary Supplement*. I'd like to thank all the editors involved, as well as Nicholas Murray of Rack Press, who suggested this book and has been its sympathetic editor. I am very grateful to Denise Riley for permission to reprint her poem 'After La Rochefoucauld', and to the Irish Poetry Shop for permission to reproduce the images from their website irishpoetryshop.wordpress.com: *ut pictura poesis*.

The Whitsun Wedding Video

1

British Poetry after Larkin: The Whitsun Wedding Video

'Wordsworth was nearly the price of me once,' said Philip Larkin in an interview with the *Observer* newspaper. 'I was driving down the M1 on a Saturday morning: they had this poetry slot on the radio [. . .] someone suddenly started reading the Immortality ode, and I couldn't see for tears. And when you're driving down the middle lane at seventy miles an hour . . .'[1]

If Larkin had careered into the hard shoulder trailing clouds of exhaust, British poetry today might look a little different. As it is, thirty years after his death from natural causes, he remains the post-war poetic monument to be – depending on your point of view – saluted on parade days or pulled down when the revolution comes.

If you live in Hull, Larkin's adopted city, his immortality has become a fact of life: there is a seven-foot bronze statue of the man at the railway station. Next year, he will be honoured in Poets' Corner at Westminster Abbey. A British poet who doesn't admire Larkin is like a politician who declines to sing the national anthem.

In a recent poem about spotting Sikh temples in the UK ('my landscape gurdwaras'), Daljit Nagra referred to his 'Larkin train-brain'.[2] Nagra's conjoined rhyme wryly acknowledges that it is difficult to write a poem about a railway journey in Britain without recalling Larkin – most famously, in his poem 'The Whitsun Weddings', which describes catching a weekend train from Hull to London filled with honeymooning couples.

In 2010, BBC Radio 3 broadcast a documentary called 'The Children of the Whitsun Weddings', featuring the poets Paul Farley and Kate Clanchy. It promised to reveal 'why and how a middle class woman and a working class man, in a train moving around a changing England, can agree unfailingly on Larkin's poems'.[3] (Nothing is more thrilling to the British than the negotiation of class differences on public transport.)

Most people, it seems, can agree on Larkin's poems, even when they are not by Larkin. In

May 2015, the *Times Literary Supplement* almost caught fire with embarrassment when a 'previously unpublished' Larkin poem turned out to be by a lesser-known poet from Hull, Frank Redpath (Redpath admired Larkin's writing, and Larkin once said that he would have been 'glad to have written' his poems).[4] The finder, a PhD student, presented a well-argued case, which persuaded the trustees of the Larkin estate and other experts. Unfortunately, nobody thought to run a few lines through Google Books.

The mistake was pointed out by Sean O'Brien, a poet who has contended in his criticism that 'no sympathy with Larkin's [right-wing] politics is required' in order to be moved by his evocation of English life.[5] The title poem of O'Brien's latest collection, *The Beautiful Librarians* (2015), attempts to reconcile the Larkinesque with left-wing politics. A nostalgic reverie about growing up in 1960s Hull, it implicitly attacks the decline of public libraries and other services under Coalition 'austerity' policies ('And all the brilliant stock was sold').[6] Larkin, by contrast, wrote a political protest poem ('Homage to a Government') about the withdrawal of colonial British troops by Harold Wilson's Labour government, 'for lack of money'.[7]

It stands to statistical reason that at least some well-known British poets must be – to use a phrase coined after the surprise majority of the 2015 General Election – 'Shy Tories'. But the explicit expression of a right-wing opinion in a poem is now rarer than a bestselling book of verse.

The presumed incompatibility of the poetic imagination and Tory politics has had Larkin's admirers wrestling with their close-readings for a long time. The most recent biography implausibly argues that the crudely anti-immigration remarks Larkin made in letters to friends were not racist at all, but the ironic performance of one of his 'provisional personae' – a horrible party hat donned to amuse friends.[8]

Geoffrey Hill, the recently retired Oxford Professor of Poetry, summed up the Larkin Problem as one of willed blindness: 'What he is seen to be in his letters he was and is in the poems.' Readers who want to ignore the implicit politics of Larkin's poetry in favour of universal truths 'overlay it with transparencies of their own preference'.[9]

Hill puts his finger here on an anxiety about poetry that runs deep in British life: where are the poems we can agree about? Modern poetry is popularly regarded as a joke. 'You'll Be Glad of a High Street Nuclear-Free Poetry Centre', chuckled the headline of a recent article by the journalist Jeremy Clarkson, who assumed this was the last thing that his readers would want to see.

Poetry nevertheless persists in our lives. The American poet Marianne Moore once wrote a poem called 'Poetry' which begins 'I, too, dislike it' – a disarming confession of something that everyone has felt ('there are things more important beyond all this fiddle'). She concludes, however, by arguing that if you like both 'the raw material of poetry' and 'that which is . . . genuine' then 'you are interested in poetry'. And that, of course, is also everyone.[10]

The real problem with much contemporary poetry is that it soft-pedals what people really like in the arts: mystery and drama. As W. B. Yeats saw it, 'popular poetry' – once, ballads; now, song lyrics – delights 'in rhythmical animation, in idiom, in images, in words full of far-off suggestion'.[11] How many modern poets have written a line that encapsulates high society as slickly as the rapper Jay-Z's 'Beautiful music when champagne flutes click'? Or a stanza as strange as this, from singer-songwriter Richard Dawson's 'The Vile Stuff'?

> My bedroom walls are papered with the stripes of
>   Newcastle United
> Between which I perceive the presence of a horse-
>   headed figure
> Holding aloft a flaming quiver of bramble silhouettes
> He is the King of Children
> Singing like a boiler: 'Tomorrow is on its way'

The genuine popularity of the current Poet Laureate, Carol Ann Duffy, is partly due to the vein of gothic melodrama that runs through her work, something she has in common with another Laureate, Ted Hughes. Unlike Hughes, Duffy has only occasionally written poems for the current Royal Family. But she was moved by the grisly spectacle of the reburial of the bones of Richard III earlier this year to compose a broken sonnet which – despite some familiar verbal padding ('lost long, forever found') – ended with one of the best lines of her Laureateship:

'as kings glimpse shadows on a battleground'.[12]

Larkin's popularity is often said to lie in his ordinariness and realism – what the critic Al Alvarez called a 'concentrated form . . . of the post-war Welfare State Englishman'.[13] This characterisation forgets how he appeals most profoundly by his strangeness. A truly 'realistic' version of 'The Whitsun Weddings' – shot from the train window on a cameraphone, say – would show us the 'uncle shouting smut' to the newly married couples boarding the train. But the end of the poem, arriving in London, can only happen the way it does in words:

> There we were aimed. And as we raced across
> Bright knots of rail
> Past standing Pullmans, walls of blackened moss
> Came close, and it was nearly done, this frail
> Travelling coincidence; and what it held
> Stood ready to be loosed with all the power
> That being changed can give. We slowed again,
> And as the tightened brakes took hold, there swelled
> A sense of falling, like an arrow-shower
> Sent out of sight, somewhere becoming rain.[14]

A disagreement broke out recently between readers of the poetry magazine *PN Review* as to whether this final stanza is 'awkward' or 'great writing'.[15] The best answer is that it is both, and that such moments of risked inarticulacy are what make Larkin so memorable. As his literary hero, Thomas Hardy, wrote, 'the whole secret of a living style' lies in 'not having too much style – being, in fact, a little careless, or seeming to be, here and there.'[16]

Hardy's secret, though, is not considered a real writing tip by a critical culture that values the abstract idea of a poem's 'craft' over the way it actually moves on the page. Last year, the political interviewer Jeremy Paxman proposed an 'inquisition' of poets, in which authors would have to explain to a public panel 'why they chose to write about the particular subject they wrote about, and why they chose the particular form and language [. . .] because it would be a really illuminating experience for everybody'.[17]

Paxman was speaking after chairing the judging panel for the annual Forward Prize, a job that will have involved reading hundreds of poems – so one can sympathise with his impatience. But when poems succeed with readers, they do so because they speak for themselves. Alice Oswald's sonnet 'Wedding' (which begins 'From time to time our love is like a sail') is now often recited at wedding ceremonies.[18] Its touchingness would not be enhanced if the assembled guests were informed that 'this sonnet begins with a line of iambic pentameter which has echoes of many conventional lines of poetry which seek to describe and define love'.[19]

To quote Frank O'Hara, a poet whose motto was 'you just go on your nerve',

> How can you really care if anybody gets it, or gets what it means, or if it improves them. Improves them for what? For death? Why hurry them along? [. . .] Nobody should experience anything they don't need to, if they don't need poetry bully for them. I like the movies too.[20]

Lyric poetry has rarely produced immediately popular art. But the poetry that people need emerges over time, and is very often by writers considered irrelevant or insufficiently ordinary by the commentators of their day. O'Hara was once patronised as a gay, coterie poet of the New

York art scene. Half a century later, part of his poem 'Mayakovsky' was recited at the end of an episode of the American TV drama, *Mad Men*, to moving effect.

This short book is about how reputations have been made in modern poetry and may be remade. In Jane Austen's *Sense and Sensibility* (1811), the favourite contemporary poet of passionate young Marianne Dashwood is William Cowper. His 'beautiful lines', she declares, have 'frequently almost driven me wild'. Readers who are led to Cowper by Marianne will, however, be surprised to find him a moderate sort on the whole, relishing picturesque pleasures but always returning home for afternoon tea – a poet, in fact, who speaks to the more sensible woman Austen's heroine will become.

Future generations may think of the present era's passion for the Northern Irish poet Seamus Heaney as akin to Marianne's for Cowper. Like Cowper, Heaney is a reflective, rural poet, moving easily between man and landscape, and finding a moral in humble objects evoked with a sumptuous accuracy of phrase (the 'small jittery promise' of seed packets, for example).[21] Like Cowper, he ironises poetry's grand manner

with conversational self-consciousness and
modest domesticity. Sonorous and memorable
as many of Heaney's lines are, it is hard to im-
agine anyone being driven wild by their care-
fully measured pleasures.

Both Cowper and Heaney are also ethically
scrupulous writers who address the wider, dark-
er world in poems that will endure among their
most profound. But they are temperamentally
poets who 'cheer but not inebriate', as Cowper
said of his cup of tea – an important kind, but
not the only kind.[22] In a hundred years, the can-
on of our times will include stronger, stranger
drink.

Poets can wait a long time for readers and
recognition. Oeuvres can be lost and restored:
recently, the seedily glittering English Sym-
bolism of Rosemary Tonks, not seen since
the 1970s. As Tom Pickard (b.1946) wrote in
his one-word-poem, 'Advice to Young Poets
(2008)':

moisturise [23]

2

A Patient Etherised upon a Tablet: The Afterlife of T. S. Eliot

O ne hundred years ago, T. S. Eliot published a poem which began:

> Let us go then, you and I,
> When the evening is spread out against the sky
> Like a patient etherised upon a table;[24]

With the bewildering simile of the third line, observed the poet John Berryman, 'modern poetry begins'.[25] It is as though 'The Love Song of J. Alfred Prufrock' has two beginnings. There is a neat rhyming couplet (I/sky), and then the metrically and logically off-beat one: the rhythm falters, the rhyme fails, and we run on into a completely new kind of poetic proposition, curbed with mock-propriety by a semi-colon.

As first-time readers, we can have no idea how such a poem is going to end, and it keeps us in this state of suspense: picking images up and dropping them; beginning and ending rhyme schemes; rhythmically advancing and retreating; and, in general, *digressing* from every expectation.

In 1915, such tendencies put Eliot's work outside the definition of poetry itself for some readers. Eliot's friend, Ezra Pound, had to persuade the editor of *Poetry: A Magazine of Verse*, Harriet Monroe, to publish the poem. When it appeared again in the book *Prufrock and Other Observations* (1917), the *Times Literary Supplement* protested:

> the fact that these things occurred to the mind of Mr. Eliot is surely of the very smallest importance to any one – even to himself. They certainly have no relation to "poetry," and we only give an example because some of the pieces, he states, have appeared in a periodical which claims that word as its title. [26]

The last time anyone asked, however – 2009 – T. S. Eliot was the Nation's Favourite Poet. And it would be an impressively perverse critic today who could seriously maintain that 'Prufrock' was not poetry of some kind. An immortal reputation can be an unhappy fate for a poet too, though, as Eliot knew. On the centenary of John Keats's death in 1921, he observed: 'All the approved critics, each in a different paper, blew a blast of glory enough to lay Keats' ghost for twenty years. I have never read such unanimous rubbish, and yet Keats was a poet.'[27]

One imagines Eliot's own ghost shivering, fifty years after his death in 1965, as his *Letters* – bulked out by reams of business correspondence – are slowly published as a series of leaden hardbacks (the latest volume takes 800 pages to get from 1930 to 1931). The complete edition of his critical prose, meanwhile, has been consigned to an online-only, subscription edition. The situation is absurd, and hardly one that Eliot – who wanted no biography, but spent much time on his brilliant and witty criticism – would have approved.

What Eliot might have wanted, though, has not been as important as what his name can sell. In 2012 Faber and Faber, the publishing firm where Eliot was a director from 1925, re-issued *The Waste Land* (1922) as an app for the iPad. This experiment in digital publishing performed a cut-and-paste job on a masterpiece of poetic collage. The manuscript facsimile of poem, featuring Ezra Pound's inspired editorial scribbling, was chopped up into an incomplete spread of page images with cursory captions. The slapdash 'gallery' of general illustrations to Eliot's 1922 poem was even less illuminating. A daytime scene of street urchins in London's East End was said to show 'where conversations like those depicted at the end of "A Game of Chess" might have taken place' – had Eliot not depicted adults talking in a pub. The line 'A crowd flowed over London Bridge' was illustrated, with wide-eyed literalism, by City workers walking to work during the General Strike of 1926. There was one picture of Eliot himself, and two of that 'heavily influenced' Eliot fan, Bob Dylan.

The electronic presentation of a work with such a rich archaeology could have been so much more ambitious and serious, to invoke just two qualities of Eliot the poet and publisher. The *Waste Land* app might have built on the example of Lawrence Rainey's *The Annotated Waste Land* (2006) by including Eliot's contemporary prose and letters; audio footnotes to the poem's musical allusions; a fully mapped scan of the manuscript. The whole thing might have been called 'iTiresias'. Instead, it was a patient etherised upon a tablet.

Eliot's original and daring qualities as a poet have not always been honoured by the annual prize that bears his name either. The T. S. Eliot Prize is administered by the Poetry Book Society, an organisation that Eliot helped to found in 1953, with the aim of sending subscribers hand-picked books of new poetry – a worthy and practical idea at a time when books were sometimes hard to obtain ('the service is undoubtedly of special benefit to those who live in isolated parts of the country, or overseas, and find it difficult to be in touch with a good bookseller').[28]

The prize automatically shortlists the four books chosen by Poetry Book Society selectors, along with six other books published in the UK that year, as decided by a panel of poet-judges. This year three of the choices are by previous winners of the prize: Mark Doty (1995), Les Murray (1996), and Sean O'Brien (2007). Rumours persist that excellent poetry is being written by poets who are not venerable names rehearsing old themes (Murray's collection is even called *Waiting for the Past*). But the PBS selectors have tended to honour established reputations and familiar modes, and the T. S. Eliot Prize judges to confirm them.

In the two decades since it began, the Eliot prize has rarely been awarded to a book that embodies the formally experimental spirit of his own *Collected Poems*. (Arguable exceptions include several book-length sequences, such as Paul Muldoon's *The Annals of Chile* (1994) and Alice Oswald's *Dart* (2001).) Last year, alongside the choice of two previous T. S. Eliot prize-winners, John Burnside (2011) and Michael Longley (2000), the PBS selectors nominated the debut of an American ex-soldier, Kevin Powers, and a book by a young Indian poet, Arundhathi Subramaniam. All lost out to *Fire Songs*, the eleventh collection by English poet David Harsent, which was described by the critic Rory Waterman as a book 'too often satisfied with unsettling readers in the most obvious of ways'.[29]

The only poet to have won the Eliot twice, Don Paterson, is also the poetry editor at Picador, a list which has recently rivalled Faber and Faber in the prize-winning stakes. Paterson celebrated his second T. S. Eliot win in 2003 with a lecture on 'The Dark Art of Poetry'. This set out clear limits to his tolerance for such things as 'poems freakishly juxtaposing archaic and contemporary registers, or mutually exclusive jargons' – a dislike that would leave *The Waste Land* on the slush pile, along with much else that Eliot admired and published.[30]

Google is not the subtlest introduction to anyone's critical thinking. But ask that search engine for images featuring 'ts eliot quotes' and the top result will be one that you have probably never heard before: 'Only those who will risk going too far can possibly find out just how far one can go.'

Quoted against stock photos of misty mountain peaks, it is an all-purpose motto for any kind of extreme leisure activity, from bungee jumping to binge drinking. But in its original context – a short preface to a volume of poems [31] – it is a serious statement of the sensibility that made Eliot the most influential poet and critic of the twentieth century, who didn't mince his words when it came to the timidity of his own times:

There is certainly, in the atmosphere of literary London, something which may provisionally be called a moral cowardice. It is not simply cowardice, but a caution, a sort of worldly prudence which believes implicitly that English literature is so good as it is that adventure and experiment involve only unjustified risk.[32]

Set against a photo of the evening spread out against the sky, this would make an inspirational screensaver for literary London a century later.

3

A Mug's Game:
The Modern Poetry Career

There is little money to be made in modern poetry. Its spin-offs, though, sometimes earn millions. In 1981, the musical *Cats* – based on T. S. Eliot's verses for children, *Old Possum's Book of Practical Cats* (1939) – opened in London and went on to run for eighteen years on Broadway. Some of the profits came back to Eliot's publishers, Faber and Faber, helping them to continue as an independent publisher with one of the most prestigious poetry lists in the world. As well as Eliot, Faber's poets include the bestselling names of W. H. Auden, Wendy Cope, Seamus Heaney, Ted Hughes, Philip Larkin, Sylvia Plath, Ezra Pound, and Derek Walcott.

The poet-publisher Eliot saw his own situation clearly. 'As things are,' he sighed during a lecture in 1933, and as fundamentally they must always be, poetry is not a career, but a mug's game. No honest poet can ever quite feel sure of the permanent value of what he has written: he may have wasted his time and messed up his life for nothing.[33]

By 'mess[ing] up his life', Eliot perhaps had in mind his own decision, as a young Harvard philosophy student, to marry, settle in England, and live by his wits – the 'penny world I bought / To eat', as he put it in his 1920 poem, 'A Cooking Egg'.[34]

Poetry is only one letter away from poverty, as several of the most original British poets of the twentieth century – Basil Bunting, W. S. Graham, Lynette Roberts – knew first-hand. W. H. Auden, their more prolific and prosperous contemporary, commented in 1962 that

The poet cannot understand the function of money in modern society because for him there is no relation between subjective value and market value; he may be paid ten pounds for a poem which he believes is very good and took him months to write, and a hundred pounds for a piece of journalism which costs him but a day's work.[35]

Poets who write book reviews in Britain to-day might think Auden's figures – which would now be approximately £200 for a poem and £2000 for a day's journalism – generous. One of the most successful poets in the country, Simon Armitage, recently managed to publish the same poem in four different places: *Stand* magazine, the *New Statesman*, the 2014 Forward Prize anthology, and his own selected poems. It was also broadcast twice on the Radio 4 programme *Poetry Please*, and will appear again in a new collection next year.

Few of Armitage's contemporaries could achieve such a feat of freelance stone-skimming. Yet the net profit probably didn't amount to more than a week or two's wages. Appropriately enough, the poem is a nightmarish description of Poundland, the budget shop to be found on every British high street, with its bright aisles of barely veiled economic exploitation ('The blood-stained employee of the month, / sobbing on a woolsack of fun-fur rugs').[36]

Other poets have found ways of adapting to the low but lucrative standards of advertisement verse. In 2011 a campaign for the gastro-pub chain Vintage Inns commissioned Sir Andrew

Motion, the former Poet Laureate, to provide lines for a promotional postcard. The poem ended with a quatrain that might have been written by a Victorian clergyman musing on the divine plan of the universe: 'All around us worlds of trouble / turn and tremble as they please. / We are rich in the fulfilment / of our vintage life at ease.'

Motion also judged a Facebook competition to write a collective poem beginning with the line 'The muted brilliance of autumn leaves'. The results confirmed that the general public's notion of poetry is still a dish served rare in the John Keats Steak House. And why not? To read or write a lyric poem is a liberating experience, one rightly associated with leisure. In Keats's own words: 'We hate poetry that has a palpable design upon us – and if we do not agree, seems to put its hand into its breeches pocket.'[37]

In the pocket of the poet's breeches, of course, is a bribe, but not one you are supposed to mention. As the poet and critic Sam Riviere has written:

Poetry has become used to positioning itself as an 'anti-commercial' mode of culture, a somehow economically untainted art form. Poetry casts itself as almost the opposite of advertising, its 'good twin', and exhibits nothing but distaste for the tactics of branding or commodification given a good deal of attention by most other contemporary art forms.[38]

Yet the copywriter's basic ingredients – emotion, wordplay, imagery – are poetic: no doubt a number of unhappy careers in verse have been averted by an advertising executive's salary. One agency recently had the canny idea of employing Pam Ayres, Britain's bestselling poet, to bring her brand of good-humoured doggerel to the animated story of a flying potato. Ayres' homely, old-fashioned persona and reassuringly rural West Country accent helped to disguise the fact that the product (a pre-baked baked potato) would once have horrified the frugal British cook.

Less inspired was the person who in 2013 unwittingly put the respected Welsh poet and clergyman R. S. Thomas on a packet of 'Hand Cooked English Crisps'. Thomas's hangdog glare had been selected from a photo archive to front a facetious competition offering 'A Fleeting Look of Contempt or £25,000'. It was quickly pointed out that Thomas, a fierce nationalist – who once contemplated with relish the ruins of an English stately home, 'the Welsh / [. . .] picnicking among the ruins / on their Corona and potato crisps' ('Plas Difancoll') – would have been mortified by such a fate.[39]

The dignity of intellectual independence is something that the uncommercial career of poetry still offers the serious-minded. Last year, Frances Leviston wrote about having turned down invitations to compose a poem for the Queen's Diamond Jubilee and take part in the Poetry Book Society's 2014 'Next Generation' promotion. 'Poets,' Leviston observed, 'especially younger poets, often face such demands of obligation and temptations of endorsement.' It is, she continued, a relief to realise 'that one need not be appointed to one's own life: that no sanctioning government, no official position, is required for the business of taking oneself seriously, in whatever sense seems right.'[40] Unlike the speaker of her cryptic poem 'Emblem', who has 'a honeybee pinned to my thumb', Leviston excuses herself from the defensive embrace of decorum and tradition:

O memory of form,
spending your sting in defence of the realm,
what medals you've become![41]

Such a position might also result in a turning-out of one's pockets, as a way of showing what poetry usually keeps hidden. This is how Sam Riviere approached the beginning of his own career as a 'Faber New Poet', in his first full collection, *81 Austerities* (2012). 'Crisis Poem', which opens the book, begins:

In 3 years I have been awarded
£48,000 by various funding bodies
councils and publishing houses
for my contributions to the art
and I would like to acknowledge
the initiatives put in place
by the government and the rigorous
assessment criteria under which
my work has thrived since 2008[42]

Riviere's ironic recitation of the bland managerial language of the arts announced an assured new voice, and the book went on to win the 2012 Forward Prize for the Best First

Collection – or, to give it its full title, The Felix
Dennis Prize for the Best First Collection.

Dennis, who died in 2014, had a career that
was the outrageous inverse of every other con-
temporary poet. Having made a fortune as a
publisher of popular magazines, he began in
later life to promote his verse with a series of
extravagant reading tours called 'Did I Men-
tion the Free Wine?' Audiences were promised
'an evening of fine French wine and poetry'.
Along the way, he managed to obtain endorse-
ments from a number of celebrities, including
Paul McCartney and Stephen Fry, for verse that
might have been written by my imaginary Vic-
torian clergyman in racier mood ('Lady, lady do
not weep – / What is gone is gone. Now sleep.
/ Turn your pillow, dry your tears, / Count thy
sheep and not thy years', 'To a Beautiful Lady
of a Certain Age').[43]

Riviere's earnings as a young poet were en-
hanced by £5,000 from Felix Dennis's fortune.
Dennis left most of the rest – a reported £500
million – to the forest that he planted in War-
wickshire: a poetic act that will outlast all his
others.

4

A Golden Age:
In Praise of Older Poets

In 1996, a BBC poll to discover the nation's favourite modern poem turned up an unexpected winner: Jenny Joseph's 'Warning'. The poem, which begins 'When I am an old woman I shall wear purple', is a light-hearted fantasy about growing less respectable with age.[44]

Around the same time it began to be reported that, with rising life expectancy, twenty-first-century Britain would see a large increase in its elderly population. Two decades later, the vigorous proliferation of poets who were born, like Joseph, before 1950, is one of the most exciting things about contemporary British verse. But it has not yet been much remarked.

Literary culture tends to celebrate youth synonymously with the 'new'. From the point of view of prize committees, the new must also not be too big or too small. The major British poetry prizes, for example, are awarded to books, not pamphlets, which means they pass over poets who don't write to the 48-page minimum required for a bound spine (the approximate length of all Philip Larkin's collections). Prizes also rarely go to a Collected or a Selected volume, which means they overlook poets who bring together publications from a number of years.

One of the single most astonishing books of poetry to appear in the UK without troubling the prize ceremonies recently was Geoffrey Hill's *Broken Hierarchies: Poems 1952–2012* (2013). Among the remarkable facts about *Broken Hierarchies* was its publisher, Oxford University Press (who officially closed their contemporary poetry list in 1999); the age of its author (81); and its length: 936 pages (Hill's earlier *Collected Poems*, in 1985, had been only 200 pages).

Since the long, confessional work *The Triumph of Love* (1999), Hill has been turning out book-length sequences at a beam-engine rate, drawing from a seemingly inexhaustible well of freshly-seen imagery and sage phrase-making. Standing on the beach in *The Orchards of Syon* (2003), for example, he finds a metaphysical moral in the movement of the waves:

Held by evidence
I say again: passion and inertia
overwhelm us, like a waste
surf compounding with its undertow.[45]

The elderly – as Jenny Joseph saw – have to
work harder to throw off the invisibility cloak
of respectability. This may be even more true
for poets than other artists. As Chris McCabe
quipped in his '101 Differences Between Poetry
and Popular Music', referring to Bob Dylan's de-
cision to use an electric guitar at a folk festival:
'No one shouted "Judas" when Geoffrey Hill
dropped the end-rhymes from his poems.'[46]

The book in which Hill exchanged end-
rhyme for free verse was *Canaan* (1996), a col-
lection with pointed things to say 'To the High
Court of Parliament' about the cash-for-ques-
tions scandal that came to symbolize the sleaze-
ridden last years of John Major's Conservative
government ('Where's probity in this – / the
slither-frisk / to lordship of a kind / as rats to a
bird-table?').[47]

Hill has now been praised as 'our greatest liv-
ing poet' by enough prominent critics, however,
to make his name one to conjure with in the

same place. In 2012, the Education Secretary, Michael Gove, when asked in the House of Commons to make a 'statement on his departmental responsibilities', replied, somewhat tangentially:

> Today is the 80th birthday of the Oxford Professor of Poetry, Professor Sir Geoffrey Hill, our greatest living poet. I am sure the whole House would like to join me in wishing him a very happy birthday, and thanking him for the fantastic work that he has done.[48]

Hansard does not record whether any Members of Parliament rose to their feet to recite a favourite poem.

Two elder poets unlikely to receive gold stars from the Secretary of State for Education are Tom Raworth (b.1938) and J. H. Prynne (b.1935). Both have been publishing since the 1960s, largely without observing the etiquette of the modern poetry career. Raworth, who left school at sixteen 'out of boredom', has parodied the kind of genteel formalism that still wins prizes:

I could go on like this all day,
Ti-tum ti-tum and doodly-ay,
And every now and then a glance
To see if I've still on my pants
And if I have, if that stain's jism
Or just a trace of modernism.

More appreciated in America than here, Raworth's latest work throws modern English into rapid, spiky, satirical patterns – a kind of poetic abstraction for which criticism on this side of the Atlantic barely has a descriptive vocabulary:

incense in helmet
pleached bonsai quincunx
fracked

in hot water

exterminating is hard work [49]

Conservative critics have always tended to dismiss linguistically disruptive poetry as the product of a pretentious muddle-headedness not worthy of serious description. Readers are

ushered away like schoolchildren from a drunk.
Former Faber poetry editor Craig Raine cari-
catures the poetry of J. H. Prynne in this way:
'The reader shouldn't expect anything in the
way of conventional "meaning" since the poet-
ry was anyway fetched up from the dark womb
of the poet's unconscious'.[50]

Anyone who sits down with Prynne's poems
after such a warning may be surprised to find
that a strongly analytical tendency animates
them. This is less surprising when one remem-
bers that the author has spent his life teaching
English Literature at Cambridge.

'Conventional' meaning is precisely the start-
ing-point for Prynne's dark, staccato explora-
tions of the sounds we make with our mouths.
His characteristic form is a rhetorical period of
bewildering referential complexity, which rhap-
sodises the attempt to think through complex
moral problems – here, the politics of environ-
mentalism:

What more can be done. We walk
    in beauty down the street, we tread
the dust of our wasted fields. The
    photochemical dispatch is im-

minent, order-paper prepared. We
    cannot support that total of dis-
placed fear, we have already induced
    moral mutation in the species. The
permeated spectra of hatred dominate
    all the wavebands, algal to hominid.
Do not take this as metaphor; thinking to
    finish off the last half-pint of milk,
look at the plants, the entire dark dream outside.[51]

Still writing with extraordinary energy in his eighth decade (see *Kazoo Dreamboats*, a verse-essay from 2011), Prynne's avant-gardism has long divided critics into uncritical camps of impatient dismissal or earnest advocacy. It is heartening to see a younger generation of readers welcome the third edition of his *Poems* (2015) with a mix of admiration and irreverence: the *London Review of Books* bookshop, for example, put up a 'Prynne-dow' featuring a series of visual tributes to his riddling images.

It sometimes seems as though our oldest poets get up in the morning in order to be irreverent. The American John Ashbery, now 88, must feel rather gloomy every time a reviewer solemnly hints at 'shades of mortality' in his later work, which is in fact steelily ageless in its queer humour. At the end of his latest book he parodies the myth of the wisely maturing poet who learns from youthful mistakes (the last line is a quotation from Keats, dead at 25):

My gosh, it's already 7:30.
Are these our containers?
Pardon my past, because, you know,
it was like all one piece.
It can't have escaped your escaped your attention
that I would argue.
How was it supposed to look?
Do I wake or sleep?[52]

The stories we tell about poets tend to stick, though. Imagine the intensely gifted Sylvia Plath had survived her suicide attempt in 1963. She would be the same age as Geoffrey Hill, and might be writing in ways quite unlike the crystalline anguish of her *Ariel* poems.

Poetry, after all, to quote Denise Riley – a philosopher who has returned to verse in her sixties after a period of silence – is song, and 'this is in some way linked to the persistence of hope'.[53] Persistence is also the theme of Riley's blank-verse, still-life lyric, 'After La Roche-foucauld':

> 'It is more shameful to distrust your friends
> Than be deceived by them': things in themselves
> Do hold – a pot, a jug, a jar, Sweet Williams'
> Greenshank shins – so that your eye's pulled
> Clear of metallic thought by the light constancy
> Of things, that rest there with you. Or without.
> That gaily deadpan candour draws you on –
> Your will to hope rises across their muteness.

Poets are not wise because they are pensionable, but because they remain watchful – with 'light constancy' – among words.

5

Full Disclosure: Criticism, the Internet, and the Future of British Poetry

Poetry critics are often tempted to play Plato. In Book Three of his political dialogue, *The Republic*, Plato has Socrates argue that the poet who is a 'sacred and wondrous pleasure-giver' should respectfully be shown out of the gates of the ideal city. 'We ourselves,' Socrates continues, 'for our own good, would employ the more austere and less pleasing poet and storyteller, who would imitate the expression of the good man and tell stories according the patterns [. . .] we laid down when educating our soldiers'.[34]

A modern version of the Platonic case against over-exciting poetry may be found in Robert Conquest's editorial introduction to *New Lines* (1956), the anthology that helped to launch Larkin as the leader of 'The Movement' poets. In the 1940s, Conquest claimed, the 'percussion' section has taken over the 'orchestra' of verse, leading to 'a rapid collapse of public taste' – a criticism implicitly directed at the most orchestral and influential British poet of the 1940s, Dylan Thomas (d.1953). In the 1950s, he continued, 'a new and healthy general standpoint' had emerged with poets such as Larkin, Thom Gunn, and Elizabeth Jennings, who wrote in a spirit of 'real . . . honesty' and refuse 'to abandon a rational structure and comprehensible language'.[55]

Conquest's ideal 'healthy' poet continues to influence the diagnosis of verse in Britain. Earlier this year, in a review for the *Guardian* newspaper, Sean O'Brien played Socratic doorman to the debut collection of the poet Jack Underwood by invoking the example of the late Irish-American poet, Michael Donaghy. O'Brien lamented that Underwood had 'renounced the implacable rigour' of Donaghy's formalism in favour of the libertinism of Frank O'Hara ('I don't even like rhythm, assonance, all that stuff. You just go on your nerve').[56]

Widening his sweep, O'Brien identified such tendencies as a 'house style' among younger poets, which he took to be symptomatic of how

in the last half-century in the west, the process of get-
ting older has ceased to necessitate (or perhaps even
permit) what would once have been thought of as
growing up – for example, in the wartime conditions
in which Keith Douglas (dead at 24) and Wilfred
Owen (dead at 26) wrote.[57]

O'Brien's logical sleight-of-hand offers the
young, dead war poets – who had to mature
unnaturally fast, under traumatic conditions –
as the exemplary 'grown-ups': the poets suited,
in Socrates' words, to the 'education of our
soldiers'.

In the days before the internet, a negative
review in a national newspaper might have at-
tracted a short letter of disagreement. Instead,
the piece drew a handful of online comments,
including one linking to a blog by a young
critic, Dave Coates, who objected, at length, to
O'Brien's 'patronising' manner with a mix of
outrage and humour ('Sir, you are 63. You are
not Melmoth the Wanderer.')[58]

Arguments about style, taste, and identity in
poetry have had to become more self-conscious
in order to be credible online. As David Wheat-
ley has written, in the one of the best surveys

available of modern British and Irish verse: 'Poetry is not free to select the conditions under which it is made today, but must explore the experience of brushing up against (or being mauled by) politics and the public sphere.' [59] The same is true of criticism. Dave Coates, for example, prefaces each of his online posts with a 'Full Disclosure' about any prior knowledge he has of the author under review. (Full disclosure: I have met David Wheatley, but not Dave Coates.)

It is, of course, possible to overstate the difference that the internet has made, or will make, to poetry. Already it seems quaint that, in 2008, a reviewer could remark that 'Frances Leviston, I think it's safe to say, is one of the few published poets with a Facebook profile.' [60] The poetic horizon in Britain has, however, widened rapidly around Larkin's vanishing train tracks this century: partly because it is now much easier to read freely among poets writing in different ways around the world, and partly because it is easier to criticise the official channels of critical taste, by – for example – reviewing a review on a blog.

Social media allow for an immediate sociology. The annual online VIDA Count campaign analyses the gender imbalance that prevails in many established trans-Atlantic literary journals, encouraging them actively to address the preponderance of male writers. The Twitter #ReadWomen campaign has also been successful in promoting neglected female writers. Introducing a much-needed new anthology of experimental women's poetry, *Out of Everywhere 2* (2015), Emily Critchley observes that it is no longer true to say (as she did in 2007) there is a 'dearth of women writing experimentally in Britain' – although it can't yet be said that many British literary journals have caught up with this trend.[61]

Similarly, the *Ten* anthologies published by Bloodaxe/The Complete Works have sought to respond to an Arts Council England report in 2005 which found that less than 1 per cent of poetry published by major UK presses was by black and Asian poets. The poet and critic Sandeep Parmar has recently described how BAME poets in the UK feel an expectation 'to assimilate to an idealised post-Movement lyric coherence' – a way of writing about their lives by which they both 'universalise and exoticise themselves'. Parmar also comments how few poets of colour are to be found among the British avant-garde, suggesting that 'experimental poetics are seen as incompatible with fixed identity politics'.[62]

One contemporary poet whose work refuses this division is Vahni Capildeo, who has written acutely about her desire to be true to the sound-world of her Trinidadian childhood:

> Moreover, the air at Deepavali hissed and rang with burnt offerings, bells, and Sanskrit (painstakingly explicated; never fully understood by me). Sanskrit had to be chanted with absolute attention to the pronunciation of each syllable, the shape and rhythm of the line, and a breath so profound the whole body resonated. We were made instruments. To this experience I can trace my instinctive revolt against such terms as 'line break', 'white space' or 'margins of silence'. Without meaning to, I developed a poetics of reverberation and minor noise.[63]

There have always been poets, like Larkin, and Eliot, who have indulged themselves in the confused poetry of cultural purity – another version of sending some kinds of people out of the gates of the city. But there have been others who saw through such vicious political fictions, such as Basil Bunting, who challenged Ezra Pound's anti-Semitism in 1938 on the grounds that every racial prejudice

> I can recall in history was base, had its foundations in the meanest kind of envy and in greed. It makes me sick to see you covering yourself with that filth. [. . .] Either you know men to be men and not something less, or you make yourself an enemy of mankind at large.[64]

Bunting's independence of vision was rewarded in old age by the advocacy of a younger generation, and he is now recognised as one of Britain's finest modernist poets. He gets the last word in this book, which is being written in September 2015, as the suffering of African and Middle Eastern refugees to Europe fills the news.

It is clear that, in the century to come, migration and climate change will remake the little island-world that Larkin cast in verse. The poetry that survives will venture beyond the love of small certainties, while embodying the hope for life that lies in the making of a poem out of the 'minor noise' of words. As Bunting wrote fifty years ago, at the end of his long poem *Briggflatts*:

> A strong song tows
> us, long earsick.
> Blind, we follow
> rain slant, spray flick
> to fields we do not know. [65]

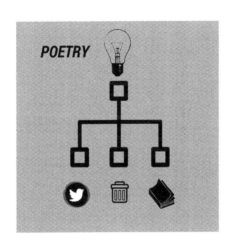

POETRY

Notes

1 Philip Larkin, *Required Writing* (London: Faber and Faber, 1983), p. 53.

2 Daljit Nagra, 'For the Domes of Britain', *The Rialto*, 83 (Summer 2015), p. 10.

3 'The Children of the Whitsun Weddings', BBC Radio 3, 22 July 2010, http://www.bbc.co.uk/programmes/booklofn.

4 Michael Caines, 'Oh Hull', *The TLS blog*, 26 May 2015, http://timescolumns.typepad.com/stothard/2015/05/oh-hull.html.

5 Sean O'Brien, *Journeys to the Interior* (Tarset: Bloodaxe, 2012), p. 17.

6 Sean O'Brien, *The Beautiful Librarians* (London: Picador, 2015), p. 29.

7 Philip Larkin, *Collected Poems* (London: Faber/The Marvell Press, 1988), p. 171.

8 James Booth, *Philip Larkin: Life, Art and Love* (London: Bloomsbury, 2014), p. 9.

9 Geoffrey Hill, 'Dividing Legacies', in *Agenda*, 34.2 (Summer 1996), pp. 27–8.

10 Marianne Moore, *The Poems of Marianne Moore*, ed. Grace Shulman (London: Faber and Faber, 2003), p. 135.

11 W. B. Yeats, 'What is "Popular Poetry"?' (1901), in *Essays and Introductions* (London: Macmillan, 1961), p. 11.

12 Carol Ann Duffy, 'Richard', *Guardian*, 26 March 2015, http://www.theguardian.com/books/2015/mar/26/richard-iii-by-carol-ann-duffy.

13 A. Alvarez, ed., *The New Poetry* (Harmondsworth: Penguin, 1966), p. 24.

14 *Collected Poems*, p. 116.

15 'Letters', *PN Review* 224 (July–August 2015), pp. 5–6.

16 Florence Emily Hardy, *The Life of Thomas Hardy 1840–1928* (London: Macmillan, 1962), p. 105.

17 'Jeremy Paxman says poets must start engaging with ordinary people', *Guardian*, 1 June 2014 http://www.theguardian.com/media/2014/jun/01/jeremy-paxman-poets-engage-ordinary-people-forward-prize.

18 Alice Oswald, *The Thing in the Gap-Stone Stile* (Oxford: Oxford University Press, 1996), p. 26.

19 'Background to the Poem', *Poetry by Heart* website, http://www.poetrybyheart.org.uk/poems/wedding.

20 'Personism: A Manifesto', in *The Selected Poems of Frank O'Hara*, ed. Donald Allen (Manchester: Carcanet, 1991), pp. xiii–xiv.

21 Seamus Heaney, *Electric Light* (London: Faber and Faber, 2001), p. 5.

22 William Cowper, *The Task* (1785), Book IV: 'The Winter Evening', ll. 36–41.

23 Tom Pickard, *hoyoot: Collected Poems and Songs* (Manchester: Carcanet, 2014), p. 46.

24 T. S. Eliot, *The Complete Poems and Plays* (London: Faber and Faber, 1969), p. 13.

25 John Berryman, 'Prufrock's Dilemma' (1960), in *The Freedom of the Poet* (New York: Farrar, Straus and Giroux, 1976), p. 270.

26 Unsigned review, *Times Literary Supplement*, 21 June 1917, p. 299.

27 T. S. Eliot, 'London Letter, May 1921', *The Dial*, 70.6 (June 1921), pp. 686–91.

28 *The Poetry Book Society: The First Twenty-Five Years*, ed. Eric W. White (1979), p. 7.

29 Rory Waterman, review of David Harsent, *Fire Songs*, 'Poetry in Brief', *Times Literary Supplement*, 27 February 2015, p. 25.

30 Don Paterson, 'The Dark Art of Poetry', http://www.donpaterson.com/files/arspoetica/1.html.

31 T. S. Eliot, 'Preface', in Harry Crosby, *Transit of Venus* (Paris: Black Sun Press, 1931), p. ix.

32 T. S. Eliot, 'London Letter, March 1921', *The Dial*, 70.4 (April 1921), pp. 448–53.

33 T. S. Eliot, *The Use of Poetry and the Use of Criticism* (London: Faber and Faber, 1933), p. 154.

34 *Complete Poems and Plays*, p. 45.

35 W. H. Auden, *The Dyer's Hand and other essays* (London: Faber and Faber, 1963), p. 84.

36 Simon Armitage, 'Poundland', *New Statesman*, 12 September 2014, p. 42.

37 John Keats to John Hamilton Reynolds, 3 February 1818.

38 Sam Riviere, 'Unlike: Forms of Refusal in Poetry on the Internet', http://pooool.info/unlike-forms-of-refusal-in-poetry-on-the-internet/.

39 R. S. Thomas, *Collected Poems 1945–1990*, (London: Dent, 1993), p. 400.

40 Frances Leviston, 'The Red Squirrels at Coole', *Harriet: A Poetry Blog'*, http://www.poetryfoundation.org/harriet/2014/10/the-red-squirrels-at-coole-by-frances-leviston/.

41 Frances Leviston, *Disinformation* (London: Picador, 2015), p. 30.

42 Sam Riviere, *81 Austerities* (London: Faber and Faber, 2012), p. 3.

43 Felix Dennis, *A Glass Half Full* (London: Hutchinson, 2002), p. 131.

44 Jenny Joseph, *Selected Poems* (Newcastle upon Tyne: Bloodaxe, 1992), p. 42.

45 Geoffrey Hill, *Broken Hierarchies: Poems 1952–2012* (Oxford: Oxford University Press, 2013), p. 376.

46 Chris McCabe, *Zeppelins* (Cambridge: Salt, 2008), p. 4.

47 *Broken Hierarchies*, p. 171.

48 HC Deb 18 June 2012, vol 546, col 587.

49 Tom Raworth, *Windmills in Flames* (Manchester: Carcanet, 2010), p. 45; Tom Raworth, *As When* (Manchester: Carcanet, 2015), p. 234.

50 Craig Raine, 'All jokes aside', *Guardian*, 11 March 2008, http://www.theguardian.com/books/2008/mar/11/poetry.thomasstearnseliot.

51 J. H. Prynne, *Poems* (Tarset: Bloodaxe, 2015), 3rd edn, p. 166.

52 John Ashbery, *Breezeway* (Manchester: Carcanet, 2015), p. 105.

53 Kelvin Corcoran, 'Interview with Denise Riley', *The Shearsman Review*, March 2014, http://www.shearsman.com/ws-blog/post/365-an-interview-with-denise-riley.

54 *Classical Literary Criticism*, trans. T.S. Dorsch and Penelope Murray (London: Penguin, 2000), p. 39.

55 Robert Conquest, ed., *New Lines* (London: St. Martin's Press, 1956), p. xi, pp. xiv-xv.

56 'Personism: A Manifesto', p. xiii.

57 Sean O'Brien, 'Happiness by Jack Underwood review – ambitious, energetic poetry', *Guardian*, 1 August 2015, http://www.theguardian.com/books/2015/aug/01/happiness-jack-underwood-review-debut-poetry-collection.

58 Dave Coates, 'Sean O'Brien on Jack Underwood – *Happiness*', 4 August 2015, https://davepoems.

wordpress.com/2015/08/04/sean-obrien-on-jack-underwood-happiness/

59 David Wheatley, *Contemporary British Poetry* (London: Palgrave, 2015), p. 161.

60 Matt Poland, 'Book Review: *Public Dream* by Frances Leviston', 15 March 2008, http://www.splicetoday.com/writing/book-review-i-public-dream-i-by-frances-leviston.

61 Emily Critchley, ed., *Out of Everywhere 2: Linguistically Innovative Poetry by Women in North America and the UK* (Hastings: Reality Street, 2015), p. 9.

62 Sandeep Parmar, 'Is Britain's poetry scene too dominated by a cultural elite?', 19 June 2015, https://news.liv.ac.uk/2015/06/19/the-liverpool-view-is-britains-poetry-scene-too-dominated-by-a-cultural-elite.

63 Vahni Capildeo, 'Letter Not from Trinidad', *PN Review*, 221 (January–February 2015), p 6.

64 Basil Bunting to Ezra Pound, 16 December 1938, quoted in Richard Burton, *A Strong Song Tows Us: The Life of Basil Bunting* (Oxford: Infinite Ideas, 2013), p. 261.

65 Basil Bunting, *Complete Poems* (Newcastle upon Tyne: Bloodaxe, 2000), p. 81.

RACK PRESS POETRY PAMPHLETS

Rack Press Editions was launched in 2014 as an
imprint of Rack Press Poetry, a poetry pamphlet press
founded in 2005, which has published over thirty
contemporary poets in quality limited editions. In
2014 Rack press won the Michael Marks Award for
poetry pamphlet Publisher of the Year.

'Rack Press ever impresses' – *Poetry Review*
'The consistently reliable Rack Press'
– *Times Literary Supplement*

Nicky Arscott
John Barnie
A. C. Bevan
Byron Beynon
Siobhán Campbell
Peter Dale
Damian Walford Davies
Martina Evans
Katy Evans-Bush
Hazel Frew
Steve Griffiths
Susan Grindley
David Harsent
Ros Hudis
David Kennedy
Anna Lewis
Philip Morre
Nicholas Murray

Katrina Naomi
William Palmer
Ian Parks
Fiona Pitt-Kethley
Ian Pople
Richard Price
Christopher Reid
Michèle Roberts
Denise Saul
Deirdre Shanahan
Róisín Tierney
Angela Topping
Dai Vaughan
John Powell Ward
David Wheatley
Dan Wyke
Samantha
Wynne-Rhydderch

From Rack Press Editions:
Nicholas Murray, *Bloomsbury and the Poets*